I AM THE
TREE OF
LIFE

By Rabbi Mychal Copeland
Illustrated by Andre Ceolin

MY JEWISH YOGA BOOK

APPLES & HONEY PRESS

AN IMPRINT OF BEHRMAN HOUSE
www.applesandhoneypress.com

This book is dedicated to my wife, Kirsti, my kids Jonah and Asher,
and the rest of my family tree. — MC

For my family, who always stood by me. To Mela, who helps me so much with
my career. And to all young readers in search of a harmonious life. — AC

Yoga teaches us to pay attention not only to our breath, but to our bodies. We challenge
ourselves, but we don't do anything that would do ourselves harm. As you go through the yoga
poses in this book, please make sure to do so safely by considering your own and the children's
physical condition and limitations and by consulting with a physician or health professional as
necessary. This book is intended as an informative guide and is not intended to replace or conflict
with any professional advice given to you and is offered with no guarantees. The authors and
publisher disclaim all responsibility and liability for any injuries or losses that may result from use
of this book or practicing the yoga poses in it.

Try it in yoga order! The poses in this book are arranged in the order of the Torah narrative.
Once you have learned the poses, try them in the flow of a more typical yoga practice: Mountain,
Crescent Moon, Star, Warrior One, Warrior Two, Downward Dog, Cobra, Child's, Tree, Dancer,
Boat, Fish, Camel, Peace.

Apples & Honey Press
An imprint of Behrman House Publishers
Millburn, New Jersey 07041
www.applesandhoneypress.com

Text copyright © 2020 by Mychal Copeland
Illustrations copyright © 2020 Behrman House

ISBN 978-1-68115-552-4

Library of Congress Cataloging-in-Publication Data
Names: Copeland, Mychal, 1970- author. | Ceolin, Andre, illustrator.
Title: I am the tree of life : my Jewish yoga book / by Rabbi Mychal Copeland ;
illustrated by Andre Ceolin.
Description: Millburn, New Jersey : Apples & Honey Press, [2020] | Includes
bibliographical references and index.
Identifiers: LCCN 2019012340 | ISBN 9781681155524 (alk. paper)
Subjects: LCSH: Judaism. | Yoga.
Classification: LCC BM45 .C66 2020 | DDC 296.7--dc23 LC record available at https://lccn.loc.gov/2019012340

Design by Alexandra N. Segal
Edited by Ann Koffsky
Printed in the United States of America

3 5 7 9 8 6 4 2

How might it feel to stand at Mount Sinai?
To dance at the Red Sea?

Let's find out. Through the yoga poses on the
pages that follow, imagine becoming a part
of these stories. Feel the stories come to life
within you.

But first take a moment to sit comfortably on
the floor. Take a deep breath in, and exhale
slowly. Repeat. Now let's begin.

I am the Tree of Life. The

TREE POSE

1) Stand straight with your arms at your sides. Feel your feet heavy
   on the ground like the roots of a tree.

2) Shift your weight onto your right foot, and raise your left heel off the ground.

3) Look ahead of you. Focus your attention on one spot, and keep
   your eyes on it to help you keep your balance.

4) Inhale as you lift your left foot up to rest on your right inner thigh (you can
   use your left hand to help pull your foot up). Breathe out and
   imagine your standing leg becoming like a tree trunk, strong and steady.

5) Bring your palms together in front of your heart. Take a deep
   inhale and slowly exhale.

6) Inhale as you raise your arms overhead. Breathe out and relax
   your shoulders. Hold the pose for another slow breath in and out.

7) Bring your arms down to your sides, your left foot to the ground,
   and repeat on the other side.

stories of the Torah come alive in me.

The Torah is called the Tree of Life.
Just as a tree is always growing and
changing, the Torah helps us grow
and change every time we read it.
A tree offers us delicious fruit,
just as the Torah offers us its wisdom.

I am the moon in the

CRESCENT MOON POSE

1) Stand with your feet together. Take a deep breath in as you bring both arms straight above your head.

2) Bring your palms together, interlace your fingers, and point upward with your index fingers.

3) As you exhale, press your left hip out to the side while you lean your arms over to the right to form the curve of a crescent moon.

4) Press your left foot into the ground, and relax your shoulders.

5) On an inhale, bring both arms back up above your head, and repeat on the other side.

night sky.

On each day of Creation, God spoke a part of our world into being. On the fourth day, God created the sun, moon, and stars.

I am the ark that saved Noah, Na'amah, their family, and the

BOAT POSE

1) Sit on the floor, with your legs bent and your feet flat on the floor.

2) Place your hands on the floor alongside your body, and lift your chest.

3) On an inhale, lean back slightly while lifting one foot off the floor, then the other. Exhale.

4) Stretch your hands out to your sides like the sides of a boat as you exhale. If you lose your balance, try placing your hands on the backs of your thighs for support.

5) After taking three deep breaths, bring down one leg, then the other, and sit up.

animals from the flood.

God warned Noah that a great flood was coming and instructed him to build a gigantic boat, an ark, that would keep his family and two of each kind of animal safe throughout the storm.

DOWNWARD DOG
(also called Tent Pose)

1) Get down on your hands and knees.
   Curl your toes under.

2) Spread your fingers wide, and push your hands down
   into the ground.

3) Exhale as you lift your knees and hips up off the
   ground, straightening your legs. Look toward your
   belly button. (Your body will be in an upside-down
   "V" position.)

4) Take a few deep breaths in and out as
   you hold this pose.

5) To come out of the pose, bring your
   knees back to the floor.

...tent that sheltered their guests.

When Abraham and Sarah spotted three tired travelers, the couple quickly invited them into their tent, offered them food, and even washed their feet.

CAMEL POSE

1) Kneel on the floor, and rest your hands on your lower back, with your fingers pointing down. Curl your toes under.

2) Arch your lower back gently as you take a breath in and lift your chest. Feel your chest lifting and rounding like a camel's hump.

3) Reach back and grab ahold of your heels if you can.

4) Hold the pose as you take three deep breaths.

5) On an inhale, place your hands on your hips and lift yourself back up to kneeling, leading with your heart and using your stomach muscles. Let your head come up last.

Rebekah's water pitcher.

When Rebekah met a thirsty traveler at the well, she showed compassion for him and poured him some water. She even offered water to his camels.

I am a star in

STAR POSE

1) Stand and place your feet wide on the floor.

2) On an inhale, raise your arms parallel to the ground at shoulder height, with palms facing down.

3) Feel your legs become strong as you press your feet into the ground.

4) Hold the pose as you take three deep breaths.

Joseph's dream.

One night, Joseph
dreamed that eleven stars
came and bowed down
to him. Many years later,
Joseph became a leader
in Egypt, and his eleven
brothers bowed before
him, just like in his dream.

I am the snake that slithered

COBRA POSE

1) Lie on the floor with your belly to the ground.

2) Place your palms on the ground alongside your chest, with your elbows pulled in toward your back.

3) As you inhale, lift your head and chest off the floor, and hiss like a snake. Straighten your arms and feel a gentle stretch in your lower back.

4) Keep your elbows close to your body.

5) Hold the pose as you take three deep breaths.

in front of Pharaoh.

When Moses demanded that Pharaoh let the Israelite slaves go free, Pharaoh stubbornly refused. Suddenly, God turned Aaron's staff into a snake. But to Aaron and Moses' surprise, Pharaoh's magicians turned their own staffs into snakes as well. Aaron's snake then swallowed theirs, showing that God was all-powerful.

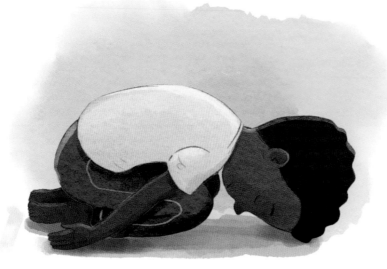

CHILD'S POSE
(also called Gratitude Pose)

1) Press your hands into the ground and push back until your stomach rests on top of your thighs, bowing to the ground.

2) Bring your arms back to rest alongside your thighs with your palms facing up.

3) Let your forehead rest on the floor, as if you are showing gratitude.

4) Relax into the pose as you take three deep breaths.

gratitude for my freedom.

When the Israelites heard from Moses that they would finally be free, they bowed their heads in thanks to God.

I am Miriam, the dancer

DANCER POSE

1) Stand with your feet together.

2) Inhale as you bend your left leg behind you, and hold the top of your left foot with your left hand. Raise your right hand overhead, and breathe as you find your balance, graceful as a dancer.

3) Exhale as you lean forward, pressing your left foot into your hand.

4) Stretch your right arm out in front of you.

5) Hold the pose as you take three deep breaths.

6) Return to standing. Drop your bent leg, and let your arms fall to your sides. Repeat on the other side.

who led the women in song.

After the Israelites left
Egypt, Pharaoh's army
trapped them at the Red Sea.
Miraculously, the waters parted
and the Israelites walked to safety on dry land.
Miriam took her tambourine and burst out in
song as she led the women in dance.

I am Sinai, the mountain where

MOUNTAIN POSE

1) Stand with your feet parallel, hip width apart. Keep your arms at your sides, with palms facing in.

2) Inhale as you lift both arms above your head, palms facing each other..

3) Exhale as you relax your shoulders.

4) Hold the pose as you take three deep breaths.

the Israelites heard the voice of God.

A thick cloud covered Mount Sinai as the people of Israel gathered around. Lightning flashed and the ground shook. A shofar blasted louder and louder as Moses climbed the mountain to receive the Ten Commandments.

I am clever Yael,

WARRIOR ONE POSE

1) Stand with your feet together.

2) Exhale and take a big step back with your right foot and point your back toes slightly off to the side. Bend your left knee so it is right above your ankle. Lift your chest up like a proud warrior.

3) Place your hands on your waist and face your hips forward. Inhale as you lift your arms overhead with palms touching and shoulders relaxed.

4) Hold the pose as you take two breaths.

5) On an exhale, bring your arms down to your sides, and step your right foot up to meet your left. Repeat the pose on the other side by stepping back with your left foot.

who fought for my people.

The prophetess Deborah had a vision that her people would be saved by a woman. Her prophesy came true when Yael used her wits and strength to defeat their enemy.

I am brave David,

WARRIOR TWO POSE

1) Stand with your feet together.

2) Take another big step back with your right foot and point your
   back toes slightly off to the side. Bend your left knee so it is right
   above your ankle.

3) Place your hands on your waist like you did for Warrior I, but this time,
   face your hips to the right.

4) Inhale and bring your arms to shoulder height so they are parallel
   to the floor, with your left arm straight in front of you and your right
   behind you.

5) Look straight ahead with a warrior's focus, past your left fingertips.

6) Take three breaths. On an exhale, bring your arms down to your sides
   and step your right foot up to meet your left. Repeat the pose on the
   other side by stepping back with your left foot this time.

who slayed the giant Goliath.

When everyone was too
frightened to fight Goliath,
the giant warrior, David
bravely stepped forward.
He threw a stone at Goliath's
forehead, and the mighty
warrior fell.

I am the giant fish that

FISH POSE

1) Lie on your back and slide your hands under your bottom, with palms facing down. Point your toes.

2) Press your hands and forearms firmly into the floor, keeping your elbows close to your sides. Lift and open your chest, with your shoulder blades pressing together. Gently arch your upper back.

3) Inhale and slowly tilt your head as if you're looking up behind you, like a swimming fish.

4) Hold the pose as you take three deep breaths.

5) To leave the pose, slowly lower your lower back to the ground, and look straight up above you.

swallowed Jonah.

God instructed Jonah to warn the people of Nineveh that
they would be punished unless they improved their behavior.
Jonah refused and ran away. He boarded a ship, but God
sent a storm and Jonah was thrown overboard. God sent a
huge fish to swallow him up and return him to dry land.

I am at peace.

PEACE POSE

1) Lie down on your back. Let your legs relax and fall open, and place the palms of your hands face up at your sides. Let your eyes close.

2) With every exhale, try to let go of your body completely and feel your weight resting on the ground.

3) Pay close attention to your breath flowing in and out of your nose. You are at peace.

שלום

The Torah is a Tree of Life, and all its paths are peace,
shalom. The word *shalom* means "whole," "complete,"
and "at peace." Your yoga practice can help lead
you to a path of *shalom*.

REFLECTION

Sit in a cross-legged position.

- How do you feel?
- Are you breathing differently than when you began?
- Do your body and mind feel calmer or more excited?
- How did becoming part of the Torah stories make you feel?
- What poses could you create for other stories you know?

WHAT'S JEWISH ABOUT YOGA?

Yoga is an ancient, physical, emotional, and spiritual practice originating in the Hindu tradition.

Movement also has an important place in Jewish practice. For example, we use movement during prayer as a way to find meaning and connection and in recognition that words are not the only way to pray.

Throughout our history, Jews have often shared ideas and spiritual traditions with people of different cultures. Combining Jewish stories with yoga practices continues that tradition of openness and sharing of ideas.